WORD
Among Us

**A Worship-centered, Lectionary-based
Curriculum for Congregations**

Learner's Guide for Young Children

Year 1

United Church Press

Cleveland, Ohio

Thomas E. Dipko	Executive Vice President, UCBHM
Ansley Coe Throckmorton	General Secretary, Division of Education and Publication
Lynne M. Deming	Publisher
Sidney D. Fowler	Editor for Curriculum Resources
Monitta Lowe	Editorial Assistant
Marjorie Pon	Managing Editor
Kelley Baker	Editorial Assistant
Lynn Keller	Business Manager
David M. Perkins	Marketing Director
Cynthia Welch	Production Manager
Martha A. Clark	Art Director
Angela M. Fasciana	Sales and Distribution Manager

Writers

Sue Quellhorst has taught in and directed nursery schools for nearly thirty years. She and her husband Ralph live in Columbus, Ohio. They have three daughters and four grandsons.

Lois Rosko grew up in India with missionary parents. She lives in Madison, Wisconsin, with her husband Bill and their three daughters. Lois is the coordinator for children's ministries at Lake Edge United Church of Christ.

Editor

Carol Wehrheim, editor for young children, is a Christian educator whose ministry is through writing and editing. She lives with her husband, Charles Kuehner, in Princeton, New Jersey.

United Church Press, Cleveland, Ohio 44115
© 1994 by United Church Press

Printed in the United States of America on acid-free paper
First printing, 1994

Design: Kapp & Associates, Inc., Cleveland, Ohio

Cover art: Mary Cassatt, *Margot Embracing Her Mother (Mother and Child)* 1902, gift of
Ms. Aimee Lamb in memory of Mr. and Mrs. Horatio Lamb, Museum of Fine Arts,
Boston. © 1993 Museum of Fine Arts, Boston. All Rights Reserved. Used by permission.

Welcome and Information Sheet

Welcome to an exciting year of exploring the Bible with your child in *Word Among Us*.

Your child will hear and explore Bible stories and passages from the lectionary readings for each Sunday. If you are in an adult group using *Word Among Us* or if the lectionary forms the basis for the service of worship for your congregation, your family will have much in common to discuss on Sundays and throughout the week.

The leaders for this group are:

Please complete the form below so the leaders of your child's group have the necessary information to make your child's experience a safe and nurturing one.

Child's name ....

Address ....

Phone ....

Birth date ....

Grade in school ....

Any allergies or health difficulties ....

Special interests ....

....

Parent(s) or guardian ....

Address ....

Phone ....

Are you members of this congregation? ....

Has your child been baptized? ....

What ways might you be able to help or share with the children?

....

....

Contents

Be Opened

Jesus did wonderful things, like helping

people hear and speak!

Mark 7:33-35

What wonderful thing
is Jesus doing?

Duccio di Buoninsegna,
Jesus Opens Eyes of Man Born Blind,
c. 1310, National Gallery of Art,
London. Used by permission.

The Bible Tells of God's Great Love

Words: Betty Doughman, 1961; alt. 1983

Music from Thomas Este's
Whole Book of Psalms, 1592

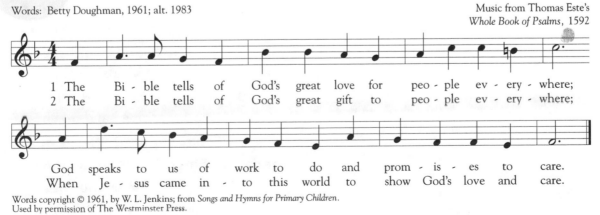

1 The Bi - ble tells of God's great love for peo - ple ev - ery - where;
2 The Bi - ble tells of God's great gift to peo - ple ev - ery - where;

God speaks to us of work to do and prom - is - es to care.
When Je - sus came in - to this world to show God's love and care.

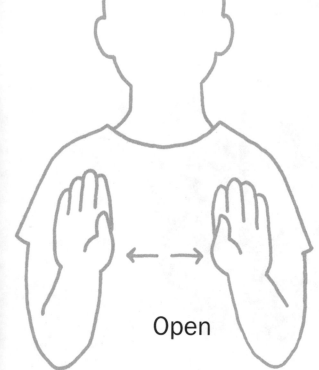

Open

Be Opened

Jesus went walking with his friends.
Walk in place or slap thighs
to sound like footsteps.

They came to the Sea of Galilee.
Spread arms wide.

**People came and gathered
round to see Jesus.**
Bring hands to chest.

**Some brought a friend
who could not hear.**
Place hands over ears.

The friend could not speak very well.
Place hands over mouth.

They asked Jesus to help their friend.
Clasp hands together, pleading.

Jesus took the friend aside.
Take a step to right or push hands to side.

**Jesus put his fingers
in the friend's ears.**
Place fingers upon ears.

Jesus touched the friend's tongue.
Place finger on tongue.

Jesus look up, sighed
Take a deep breath.

and said, " Ephphatha (Ef'e tha)."
Look up.

That is, "Be opened."
Place both open hands side by side,
and draw them apart in an arching movement.

The friend could hear.
Cup hands over ears.

The friend could speak.
Cup hands over mouth.

All the people gathered around.
Bring hands to chest.

**They shouted, "Jesus does
wonderful things, like helping people
hear and speak."**
Wave arms joyfully.

✳ *at* Home

✳ The children will learn the signs for an important
✳ word in the story during these Pentecost Sundays.
Enjoy using the sign at home.

✳ Have your child imitate your actions as you tell the
Bible story. Young children learn through repetition.
✳ You can help your child learn the story by saying it
together.

✳ The refrain on side one will be sung many times
over the course of this year. Singing them with your
✳ child will tell your child that what is learned in
church school is important at home too.

Teach and Be Taught

God wants us to listen and learn.

Isaiah 50:4-5a

Can you tell a story about this picture?

What bright and beautiful things do you see?

All Things Bright and Beautiful

Music: English melody, 17th century   Words: Cecil Frances Alexander, 1848; alt.

All things bright and beau - ti - ful, all crea - tures great and small,

All things wise and won - der - ful, our dear God made them all.

Music arrangement copyright © 1965 by Graded Press.

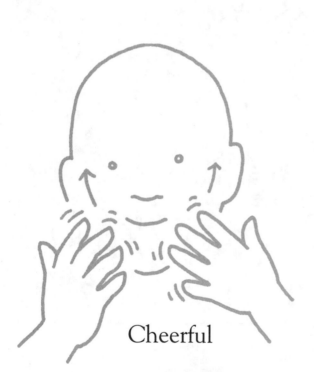

Cheerful

▶ *at* **Home**

▶ Use this sign as you and your child speak of your delight in the world around you.

▶ Begin your day with this prayer.

▶ Praise the cheerful things that are said in your home. Let your child teach you about seeing, hearing, tasting, and touching. Rejoice together in the wonders of God's creation.

▶

▶

God Gave Me a Mouth

God gave me a mouth to say
  Cheerful words every day.
God gave me ears to hear
  And every morning, I can't wait
  To wake my ears to something new.
God has taught me to listen and learn
  That God is near and cares for me.

Good Morning, God

Good morning God, What a beautiful day!
I want to start learning right away!
Wake up my ears. Wake up my nose.
Wake up my fingers. Wake up my toes.
Wake up my eyes. Wake up my head.
Wake up my legs and I jump out of bed.
I'm all woke up from head to toe.
Help me to learn what I should know.
Amen.

12

Welcome the Children

Jesus welcomes children.

Mark 9:35-37

Emil Nolde, *Christ Among the Children*,
1910. Gift of Dr. W. R. Valentiner,
The Museum of Modern Art,
New York. Used by permission.

Can you tell a story about Jesus and a child?

Good Day

Buenos días (bwaynohss deeahss) - *Spanish*
Jambo - *African*
Guten tag (gooten tahgg) - *German*
Kon-nichiwa - *Japanese*
Zdrástvuyte (zdrahstvuyteh) - *Russian*
Kahlee-maira - *Greek*
Tere (terreh) - *Estonian*
Buon giorno (bwawn jorrno) - *Italian*
God dag (goodah) - *Swedish*

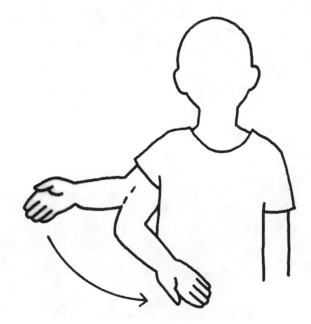

Welcome

✳ *at* **Home**

✳ Talk with your child about ways you prepare
for and welcome guests. Invite a family from
✳ your congregation for dessert. Involve your
child in preparing for their visit as you clean
✳ the house and make the dessert. Learn the
sign for "welcome" or "good day" in another
✳ language to use as you greet your guests.

✳

Deeds of Power

John came to Jesus when he
needed to talk to someone.

Mark 9:38-41

Help Me, O God

Words: Lois Rosko, 1993

Music: Thomas Tallis, c. 1567

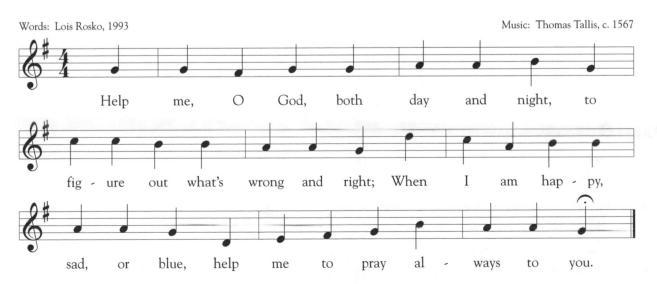

Help me, O God, both day and night, to
fig-ure out what's wrong and right; When I am hap-py,
sad, or blue, help me to pray al-ways to you.

James 5:13-16

Are you troubled? Pray.
Are you cheerful? Sing happy songs of praise.
Are you hurting? Go to a friend who can help you.
     Together you can pray for the hurt to stop.
When you make a mistake,
     say "I'm sorry" in prayer
     and to the person you hurt.
Pray for yourself and for one another.
Prayer can be very powerful.

Pray

Help Me to Pray

When we are feeling bad, **God, help me to pray.**

When we are glad, **God, help me to pray.**

When we are mad, **God, help me to pray.**

When we play, **God, help me to pray.**

When we laugh, **God, help me to pray.**

When we cry, **God, help me to pray.**

When I make a mistake, **God, help me to pray. Amen.**

at Home

Perhaps the sign for "pray" can become a signal for you and your child that you are praying for one another.

Develop a routine for daily prayer with your child. Pray together during glad times, or mad times, or feeling bad times.

Today the children learned about prayer and times when they can talk with God. Use "James 5:13-16" and "Help Me to Pray" to continue that learning at home.

The Work of God's Fingers

I see the work of God's fingers all around me.

Psalm 8:3-5

We enjoy
God's creation.

We care for God's world together.

O How Glorious, Full of Wonder

Words: Curtis Beach, 1958

Music: Traditional Dutch melody

O how glo-rious, full of won-der is God's name in all the earth.

Copyright © 1958 by The Pilgrim Press, 700 Prospect Avenue, Cleveland, OH 44115. Used by permission.

★ *at* **Home**

★ Explore God's creation and wonder together. Encourage the creativity of your child, the creativity given each of us by God.

★ Rejoice in your own creation as you and your child sing "O How Glorious, Full of Wonder" or move to "Psalm 8." Let your child help you discover the awesome nature of God and all that God created.

★

★

17

Glory

Psalm 8

O God, Our God

Over all the earth

You are totally awesome.

Your glory sings out beyond

the heavens.

Children, even babies, sing praise to you.

When I look up into the sky

and see what your fingers havemade

Like the moon

and the stars.

Sometimes I feel very small and wonder

How can you know I'm even here?

But you made me very special

You touched me with your glory.

You have given me a special job, too

To care for this wonderful world with you

O God, Our God

Over all the earth

You are totally awesome.

Gracious Justice

Seek good.

Amos 5:14-15

The Amos Rap

One day Amos went into town,
To the busiest part. Everyone was around.
Old Amos got up and began to shout.
"I want to tell you what **God** is mad about.
Hey! Listen to me! O people of **God!"**
But nobody stopped. So, Amos got loud.
"Listen to what **God** has to say.
God does not want us to live this way.
You push each other. You do not share.
You're just being mean everywhere.
Don't look to be bad. Look for ways to be good.
Help each other. And live as you should.
Live God's way each and every day
Be God's helper, that's what I say.
Live God's way each and every day.
God will be with you all the way.
Yes, **God will be with you all the way."**

Live **God's way** each and **every day,**
God will be with you **all the way.**

We Love Because God First Loved Us

Words and music: Mary Duckert, 1978

We love be-cause (We love be-cause) God first loved us. (God first loved us). the Son of God (The Son of God) has shown us how. (has shown us how). We love be-cause (We love be-cause) God first loved us. (God first loved us). And so we are (And so we are) God's chil-dren now. (God's chil-dren now.)

Help

Add this sign to the others that you and your child have learned. Make up games with them.

at Home

Celebrate ways your child helps. Plan ways that you and your child can help a neighbor or friend.

"We Love Because God First Loved Us" is an echo song. Young children enjoy a song when they can copy what you sing, or later you can copy what they sing. During future lessons, we will substitute other words for "love," such as "serve" or "help." You and your child can try other words as well.

True Greatness

To be great, we must serve others.

Mark 10:42-45

Who are people that you can help?

How do you serve at home?

▶ *at* **Home**

▶ Name the ways your child is a special helper. Your child is learning that to be a follower of Jesus is to serve and help others. Look for opportunities for your child to help you, such as helping you set the table for dinner or going with you to visit an elderly person.

▶ The hand rhyme, "Helping Jesus," includes most of the signs the children have learned thus far. When you and your child do it together, praise your child for having learned these signs. Talk together about what the words mean and how the signs help you understand the words.

21

Helping Jesus

James and John said one day,

"Jesus, please do things our way.

In your glory, let us sit

As close to you as we can get."

"I need helpers at my table."

Jesus asked, "Are you able?"

"Come, serve others as I do.

Welcome, welcome all of you."

Serve

22

A Great Company

We are part of all God's people.

Jeremiah 31: 8-9a

Can you add yourself to this picture?

For young children, mercy means love.

Jeremiah Speaks

The prophet Jeremiah long ago proclaimed this word of God.
Sing aloud with gladness.
Shout with joy to God.
What a great group of people gather in God's name!
All kinds of people young and old.
People who are hurting and people who are well.
What a great group of people gather in God's name!
God will lead them.
God will help them.
What a great group of people gather in God's name!

Paraphrase of Jeremiah 31:7-9

Wherever Love Is, God Is There Too

Wherever love is

God is there, too.

God is in me

'Cause I love you

Wherever love is

God is there too

God is wherever love is.

Brian C. Sirchio. Crossroad Ministries.
Used by permission.

❤ *at* Home

We all find ourselves in great company as described by Jeremiah. Sometimes we are joyful; at other times we are sad. The same is true for young children. As your child learns to name the emotions inside, you can help him or her understand that God accepts us any way we are.

A good way for your child to learn of God's acceptance is to observe and take part in your acceptance of others. With your child, help someone who may be lonely or ill. Show God's mercy to all.

All Your **Heart**, All Your **Soul**, All Your **Mind**!

Love God.

Mark 12:28-31

When we show love

to others,

it can be like showing

them something of

God's love.

Jesus' Teaching

Love

We can learn to love God 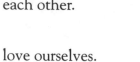 with all our heart.

We can learn to love God with all our mind.

We can learn to love God with all our strength.

We can learn to love each other.

We can even learn to love ourselves.

▶ *at* **Home**

▶

▶ Sit together. Talk about what it might feel like to have God hug you.

▶ Talk of God's love and ways to show that love.

▶ We used this prayer at snack time, and we hope you will use it at home:

▶
▶
▶
▶
▶

▶
▶
▶ **God is great. God is good,**
▶
▶ **and we thank God for**
▶
▶

▶
▶
▶

Amen.

▶
▶
▶
▶

Fullness of the Gift

The poor woman put in everything she had,
all she had to live on.

Mark 12:41-44

Give

The woman who had almost nothing
gave all she had to God's temple.

We Give God All We Can

Music: SCHUMANN, from Mason and Webb's *Cantica Laudis*, 1850.

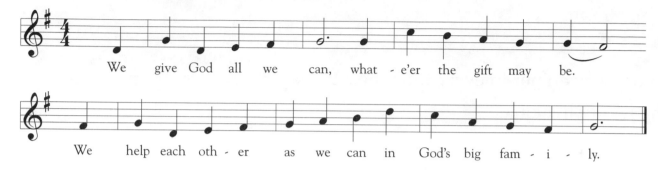

We give God all we can, what-e'er the gift may be.

We help each oth-er as we can in God's big fam-i-ly.

at **Home**

Prayers of thanksgiving are the first prayers we teach young children. You can help your child learn to give thanks by modeling as you give loving thanks to one another.

Give loving thanks to God:

—in prayer.

—with a food offering to the food pantry.

—with regular offering.

How else can you give to God?

God Among Us

God is always with me.

Psalm 16:5-8

Psalm 16

O God, there are times
>I would like a big hug.
>It would remind me of your goodness.
>I have a hard time being good without you.

You give me food and drink.
>You give me what I need.

You are like a loving, caring friend.
>You give me love.

You are like a teacher.
>You help me learn new things.

You are with me and help me, even at night.
You are always with me
>and it makes me glad.

When I'm aware of you I feel goodness
that never goes away.

at **Home**

Celebrate God's presence with songs of thanks. Sing the songs your child has learned in church school when you are riding together in the car or walking in the park. Help your child practice talking with God, particularly at bedtime and at mealtime. Look for other times you and your child can express your thanks to God as well.

God is With Me

God is up above.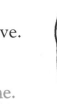

 God is with me.

God is far below.

God is with me.

God is at my side.

God is with me.

God is in front of me.

God is behind me.

God is all around me.

God

 God is with me.

30

I Bring the Truth

I came into the
world to testify
to the truth.

John 18:37-38

Can you find Jesus
in this picture?

Pietro Lorenzetti, *Christ Before Pilate*, 1335,
Pinacoteca Vaticana, Cittá del Vaticano, Italy
(Art Resource, N.Y.). Used by permission.

Psalm 93

God is full of majesty and strength.
God began the whole world from the
very beginning.
The waters of the seas lifted and roared.
The waters of the seas made gigantic waves.
But God is more powerful than
the biggest waves.
And God is forever! Praise God!

Jesus' Prayer

Our Father [and Mother],

Who is in heaven,

Holy is your name.

Your world come.

Your will be done

On earth, as it is in heaven.

Amen.

▶ *at* **Home**

▶ Read Psalm 93 as retold here and act out
things on earth that God rules over.

▶ Be the ocean, a tall tree, a whale, an
elephant, a tiny ladybug, or a rose bush.

▶ Pray the portion of Jesus' prayer together. Do
not attempt to teach the entire prayer to your
young child. That can come later. This much
of the prayer will allow your child to feel
more a part of the service of worship or any
occasion when the prayer is prayed out loud.

Behold the **Signs**

Jesus said, "There will be signs in the sun, the moon, and the stars, and on the earth."

Luke 21:25a

An Advent Prayer
from Psalm 25:4-5

Help us know your ways, O God.
Teach us your paths.
You are our hope.
We wait for your coming.
Amen.

Jesus is our **star** of hope!

Glo — ri - a in ex - cel - sis De - o, Glo — — ri - a in ex - cel - sis De - o.

The movements for the song derive from the sign for "glory" that the children learned in Pentecost 1. Start crouched down. Clap on "glo" of gloria. Slowly raise the right hand in an arc reaching higher and higher, ending on tiptoe. During "in excelsis deo" extend the left hand up, so both hands are reaching up. Repeat each time the phrase is sung.

33

Pray the **Advent Prayer** together.

Sing or speak the words and move to "There's a Song in the Air!" using the directions below. If you have a recording of the carol, play it after you have practiced the movements.

There's a Song in the Air!

Stand in a circle.

There's a song in the air!	Sweep hands over head from left side to right and a step to the right.
There's a star in the sky!	Sweep hands over head right to left and step to the left.
There's a mother's deep prayer	Stoop down and touch the ground with both hands.
And a baby's low cry!	Rock back and forth
And the star gives us hope while the beautiful sing,	Stand and skip to the right.
For the manger of Bethlehem cradles the King!	Skip to the left.

Josiah G. Holland. Used by permission of Charles Scribner's Sons. Modified 1994. Used by permission.

▶ *at* **Home**

Plan a time for family worship during Advent. Make a circle of greens, real or artificial, for an Advent wreath. Stand the star your child brought home in a lump of clap or play dough hidden in the wreath. Do not place the star in the Advent wreath if you have candles that you will light in it.

Good News! Jesus comes to show God's love!

Prepare the Way

Prepare the way of the Lord.

Luke 3:4b

Frans Pourbus the Elder,
Sermon of St. John the Baptist,
Musée des Beaux-Arts,
Valenciennes, France
(Photographie Giraudon/
Art Resource, N.Y.).
Used by permission.

John the Baptist was a prophet and messenger of God who

prepared the way for Jesus. Where is he in this picture?

John's Message

"Good news! Jesus is coming, Prepare the way!
Good news! Jesus is coming, Prepare today!
Good news! God loves us all. Hooray! Hooray!
Good news! Jesus will show us God's love. Hooray!"

at **Home**

Today we talked about preparing for Jesus' birth. Talk with your child about the ways your family is preparing to celebrate the coming of Jesus. Your child will probably have some suggestions from our conversation. The yarn ornament we made today is called an *ojo de Dios* or eye of God. It reminds us that God's love wraps us as the yarn wraps the sticks, holding them together. Place it in a lump of clay or play dough in the Advent wreath.

For your family Advent worship, use the Advent Prayer from the learner's guide for Advent 1 and the following dance to "Go, Tell It on the Mountain." Joyful shouting of the good news was also what John the Baptist did.

Go, Tell It On The Mountain (spiritual)

Go, tell it on the mountain,   Hold hands to mouth and move them outward

Over the hills and everywhere,   Swoop one hand high over the other

Go tell it on the mountain   Same motion as first line

That Jesus shows God's love.   Hug one another

Rejoice!

Rejoice in Jesus always; again I will say, Rejoice. Let your gentleness be known to everyone. Jesus is near.

Philippians 4:4-5

Rejoice!

God's peace is with you!

An Advent Prayer

God, we thank you.
We thank you that we can ask you
    to help us.
We thank you that we can learn
    about all that you have done.
We thank you that we can tell
    others about all you have done.
God, you are really great and
    full of glory.
Everyone should sing of your glory.
    Amen.

Place the joy stick your child made today in your Advent wreath.

Today the children made mini-posters on the theme of rejoicing. We suggested that they give them to someone who needs comfort and joy. Talk with your child about who might receive the mini-poster and how it can be delivered.

During your Advent family worship, pray the Advent prayer on this learner's guide. Dance the following carol.

God Rest You Merry, Gentle Folk

Form a circle.

God rest you merry, gentle folk

Join hands and take four steps to the right.

When you're at work or play.

Take four steps to the left.

Remember Christ our Savior

Take four steps to the right.

Was born on Christmas Day.

Take four steps to the left.

To let us know God loves us all

Take three steps toward the middle of the circle.

And bring God's peace today.

Take three steps back.

O great news of comfort and joy,

Stoop down and stand, reaching up.

Comfort and joy!

Sway from the waist to the right and then to the left.

O great news of comfort and joy

Stoop down and stand, reaching up.

Blessed

In those days Mary set out and went with haste to a Judean town in the hill country, where she entered the house of Zechariah and greeted Elizabeth. When Elizabeth heard Mary's greeting, the child leaped in her womb. And Elizabeth was filled with the Holy Spirit and exclaimed with a loud cry, "Blessed are you among women, and blessed is the fruit of your womb."

Luke 1:39-42

Elizabeth greeted Mary with great joy.

Giotto di Bondone, *The Meeting of the Virgin and Elizabeth*, fresco, after 1306, la capella degli Scrovegni (Arena Chapel), Padua, Italy (Alinari/Art Resource, N.Y.). Used by permission.

Mary's Song to God

God is so good!
The Mighty One has blessed me!
God blesses those who are down—they are lifted up.
God blesses those who are too high—they are brought down.
God blesses those who are hungry with good things to eat.
God blesses those who have much—they are shown how to share.
Thanks be to God, who makes things come out right.
God blesses us all.

{ Make up a song to go with Mary's words. Perhaps you can make up movements to go with your song. }

Can you tell a story about this picture

Who are the persons in it

What is happening

Angels We Have Heard on High

Join hands.

Angels we have heard on high,

> *Take four steps forward, raising your arms as you move.*

singing sweetly through the night,

> *Take four steps back, lowering your arms at the same time.*

And the mountains in reply,

> *Take four steps to the right, raising your arms as you move.*

Echoing their brave delight.

> *Take four steps to the left and lower your arms.*

Glo-

> *Stoop and slap the floor on "g."*
> *Wiggle the fingers of your right hand as you raise it high.*

ria

> *Stand on tiptoes to reach higher with your right hand.*

in excelsis deo!

> *Raise and extend your left hand as high as you can.*

Gloria in excelsis Deo!

> *Repeat movements for "Gloria in excelsis Deo."*

at Home

Along with the story about Elizabeth and Mary, the children heard the story of Jesus' birth. During these days before Christmas, enjoy the story of the nativity with your child daily. Read it from a children's Bible storybook or tell it in your own words.

Today your child made a paper chain as a reminder that Jesus brought God's love to bring us together. Place the chain on your Advent wreath. As a family you may want to add more links to the chain and use it as a decoration.

In your Advent and Christmas family worship, use Mary's song, the message from the angel, the Advent prayer, and the dance to "Angels We Have Heard on High." Your child has been learning the refrain from this carol during Advent.

An Advent and Christmas Prayer

God, you have given us many good things.
Thank you for Jesus, your special gift to us all. Amen.

Glory to God!

And suddenly there was with the angel a multitude of the heavenly host, praising God and saying, "Glory to God in the highest heaven, and on earth peace among those whom God favors!"

Luke 2:13-14

Henry Ossawa Tanner, *Angels Appearing Before the Shepherds*, 1910, National Museum of American Art, Smithsonian Institution, Washington, D.C. (Art Resource, N.Y.). Used by permission

"Do not be afraid! I bring good news.

I bring good news of great joy for all people.

Jesus is born this day in Bethlehem.

You will find baby Jesus, wrapped in cloth,

lying in a manger."

Sing A Different Song

Words and music: The Iona Community, 1987

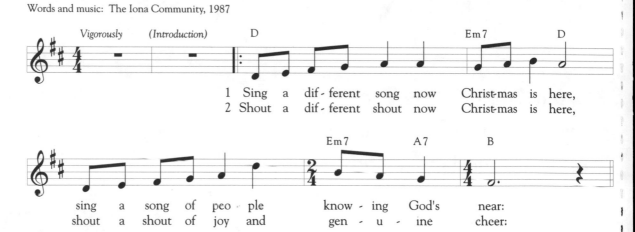

Vigorously   (Introduction)

1 Sing   a   dif - ferent   song   now   Christ-mas   is   here,
2 Shout a   dif - ferent   shout now   Christ-mas   is   here,

sing   a   song   of   peo - ple   know - ing   God's   near:
shout a   shout of   joy   and   gen - u - ine   cheer:

A Christmas Prayer

Happy birthday, Jesus.
May the whole world sing glory
to you in a big, big way!
Amen! Amen!

at Home

What an exciting time for children! As your family enjoys the festivities of Christmas, set aside time for thanking God for the birth of Jesus. Sing "Happy Birthday" to Jesus and pray the Christmas prayer together.

Invite your child to tell the story of Jesus' birth with you. Begin the story and have your child fill in when you stop.

Jesus, Amazing child

After three days Mary and Joseph found Jesus in the temple, sitting among the teachers, listening to them and asking them questions. And all who heard him were amazed at his understanding and his answers.

Luke 2:46-47

Jesus Among the Teachers, Vie de Jesus Mafa, 24 rue du Marechal, Joffre, 78000 Versailles, France. All rights reserved. Used by permission.

This is how one artist thought Jesus and the teachers in the temple looked. What do you think the teachers are thinking? What do you think Jesus is thinking?

Jesus grew strong and wise.

Psalm 148

(tune: Old Hundredth)

Praise God, all things in sky and sea.
Praise God, all creatures wild and tame.
Praise God, all people, faithfully.
Let all things praise God's holy name.

at **Home**

Little is known about Jesus' childhood. But we are told that he grew "in wisdom and years."
Your child is growing in the same ways. You have an important role to play in that growth.

Try to find time to continue a regular routine of family worship. Sing "Psalm 148." Tell your child a story
from the Bible. Wonder together about the parts of the story that aren't in the Bible. Think about how the
persons in the story felt. Help your child to gain an appreciation for the Bible that will last for a lifetime.

 **Jesus, his family, and many other families
traveled to Jerusalem for the Passover festival.
Along the way, they sang songs praising God.
What song that praises God do you know?**

Jesus Baptized

Now when all the people were baptized, and when Jesus also had been baptized and was praying, the heaven was opened, and the Holy Spirit descended upon him in bodily form like a dove. And a voice came from heaven, "You are my Child, the Beloved; with you I am well pleased."

Luke 3:21-22

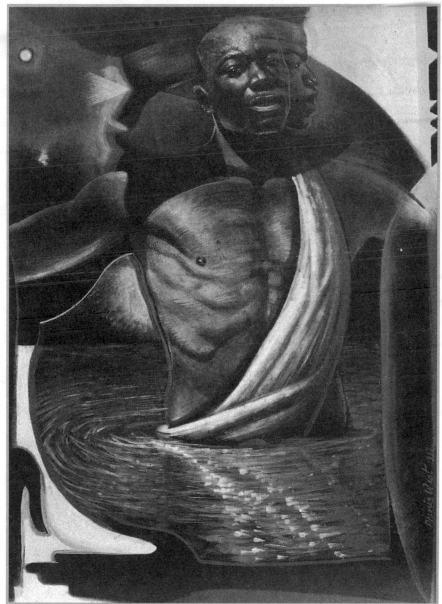

Pheoris West, *The Baptism of Jesus Christ*, artist's collection, Columbus, Ohio. Used by permission.

"You are my child, whom I love very much."

★ ★ ★ ★ ★ ★ ★ ★ ★ ★ ★ ★ ★ ★ ★ ★ ★

When Jesus

When Jesus was **baptized,**

things began to change.

A dove came down and a voice did say,

"This is my child. Listen. Obey."

When Jesus was baptized,

things began to **change.**

at **Home**

The story of the baptism of Jesus presents an opportunity to talk with your child about her or his baptism or your own baptism. Get out the photograph album, slides, or video. Recall your special feelings.

Because we know we are in God's family, we know we can pray to God at any time. Pray the prayer on this learner's guide with your child in the morning before you begin the day.

Prayer

God, we thank you for the night

And for the pleasant morning light,

For rest and food and loving care

And all that makes the world so fair.

Amen.

Little Children, Welcome

Words: Fred Pratt Green, 1973   Music: Roy Hopp, 1988

Lit - tle chil - dren, wel - come! Earth is yours to live in;

arms of love pro - tect you, lit - tle chil - dren, wel - come!

the Wedding at Cana

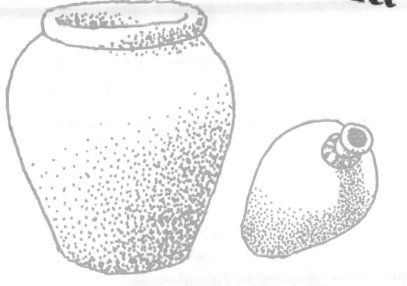

Jesus changed water
into wine,
the first of his signs,
in Cana of Galilee.
He revealed his glory;
and the disciples
believed in Jesus.

John 2:11

The Peasants of Solentiname, *Untitled (Jesus at Cana)*, as reproduced in
The Gospel in Art by the Peasants of Solentiname, ed. Philip and
Sally Scharper (Maryknoll, N.Y.: Orbis Books). Used by permission.

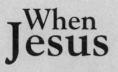

When Jesus

When Jesus went to **parties**,
  things began to change.

Water turned to tasty drink.

People asked, "What *do* you think?"

When Jesus went to parties,
  things began to **change.**

≋ *at* **Home**

Joyfully celebrate God in our midst! Sing songs of praise! Dance with your child. Celebrate God's wonderful gift of life and love. Give thanks to God with the prayer based on Psalm 36 on this learner's guide.

Prayer Based on
Psalm 36:5-10

Your love, O God, goes up to the heavens.

  (Raise arms straight up.)

Your love goes beyond the clouds in the sky

  (Move arms slightly apart.)

Your goodness is bigger than the mighty mountains

  (Move arms straight out to sides.)

Your care goes deeper than the deepest sea.

  (Stoop down and bring hands to floor.)

You care for all animals and all people.

  (Stand up and join hands.)

Everyone can gather and eat at your table.

  (Hands joined, move them in slightly.)

Everyone can drink your joy and delight.

  (Hands joined, move them up to shoulder height.)

We come to your table with thanksgiving.

  (Hands joined, move them above head.)

Help us to do what is right. Amen.

  (Let go of hands; place hands to chest.)

Fulfilled in Your Hearing

Jesus stood up to read . . .
"The Spirit of God is upon me,
because God has anointed me
to bring good news."

Luke 4:16c, 18

Rembrandt van Rijn, *Christ Preaching*, 1656, Metropolitan Museum of Art, New York. Used by permission.

This is my **job.**

This is what God **wants me to do.**

When Jesus

When Jesus started **working,**
  things began to change.

  So all could feel

God's love was real,

  When Jesus started working,
  things began to **change.**

Luke 4:18-21
(Isaiah 61:1-2)

God has
  Stretch arms up and out.

chosen me:
  Bring hands into self.

To change things
  Tumble hands.

So all can see
  Point to eyes.

God's love
  Cross hands at wrist and press to heart.

And glory.
  Clap right hand on the left and lift right hand
  into arch in front of you; shake the fingers as
  you move it.

To cheer, and free, and help each one
  Smile broadly.

To live like God's daughter or son.
  Stand proudly.

Prayer Based on
Psalm 19:14

Let what we say
Move hands from mouth as if
words are flying out

And what we feel in our hearts
Hold your hands over heart.

And what we do
Slide hands from toes to top of head.

Fit together in your plan, O God,
Hold hands in a circle.

To show everyone your love.
Still holding hands, lift them up.

Amen.
Gently squeeze your partner's hands
and drop hands.

at **Home**

Talk about ways you help show God's love in your work, in your home, at church, and other places. Plan times when your child can participate in these ministries. Children of all ages learn about being Christian by taking part in Christian ministry. Learning by doing is especially important for young children. Include your child when you deliver flowers to a sick member of your congregation, or pray for a family who is moving away. Knowing that you care about others assures your child of your care for her or him too.

Accept or Reject

And Jesus said, "Truly I tell you, no prophet is accepted in the prophet's hometown."

Luke 4:24

When Jesus **talked** to people, things began to change.

Some were glad,

But some got mad.

When Jesus talked to people, things began to **change.**

Prayer Based on 1 Corinthians 13

I may know lots of fancy words,	Point to mouth.
but without your love they mean nothing.	Dust hands off once.
Teach us, God, your love.	Start crouched low and jump up.
I may be smart and know a lot,	Point to head.
but without your love I know nothing.	Dust hands off once.
Teach us, God, your love.	Start crouched low and jump up.
I may be the strongest one around,	Flex biceps.
but without your love, it does no good.	Dust hands off once.
Teach us, God, your love.	Start crouched low and jump up.
Love is patient. Love is kind.	Cross hands on chest.
Love is the best thing you can find.	Spread hands out and up.
Teach us, God, your love.	Start crouched low and jump up.

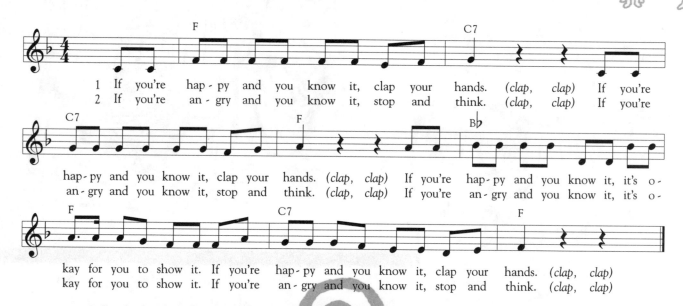

1 If you're hap-py and you know it, clap your hands. (clap, clap) If you're
2 If you're an-gry and you know it, stop and think. (clap, clap) If you're

hap-py and you know it, clap your hands. (clap, clap) If you're hap-py and you know it, it's o-
an-gry and you know it, stop and think. (clap, clap) If you're an-gry and you know it, it's o-

kay for you to show it. If you're hap-py and you know it, clap your hands. (clap, clap)
kay for you to show it. If you're an-gry and you know it, stop and think. (clap, clap)

1. For the first stanza, replace "clap your hands" with other phrases using other body parts in nonhurting ways, such as: "give a smile," "stomp your feet," "laugh out loud."

2. For the second stanza, replace the phrase "stop and think" with other ways to express anger positively, such as: "talk it out," "run around," "give a frown."

Words for stanza two by Camy Condon and James McGinnis in *Helping Kids Care*. The Crossroad Publishing Company, 1987. Used by permission. Music from *Making Music Your Own–K* © 1966 Silver Burdett Company. Used by permission.

☺ at **Home**

Among so many things, young children are learning to identify and express feelings. This story with its strong feelings provided an opportunity to talk about helpful things to do when we are upset or angry.
Sing "If You're Happy" found on this learner's guide. Talk with your child about alternatives to violence. Censor your own language and actions. It's never too soon nor too late to eradicate violence from our lives.

Do Not Be Afraid

But when Simon Peter saw the boats filled with fish, he fell down at Jesus' knees, saying, "Go away from me, Lord, for I am a sinful person!" … Then Jesus said to Simon, "Do not be afraid; from now on you will be catching people." When they had brought their boats to shore, they left everything and followed Jesus.

Luke 5:8, 10b-11

Raphael (Raffaello Sanzio), *Miracle of the Fishes*, tapestry, The Tapestry Gallery, Vatican Pinacoteca (Scala/Art Resource, N.Y.). Used by permission.

When Jesus

When Jesus **talked** to people,
    things began to change.

"I can see the good in you.

You can be God's helper too."

    When Jesus talked with people,
things began to **change**.

Let's just try!

53

Prayer Based on Psalm 138

Thank you with all our hearts,

Thank you, God, thank you.

Thank you for your love,

Thank you, God, thank you.

Thank you for listening to us,

Thank you, God, thank you.

Thank you that you help us,

Thank you, God, thank you.

Thank you that you made us just the way we are.
Keep us in your care.

Thank you, God, thank you.

Sometimes I Feel **Small**

Sometimes I feel small

And think I cannot help at all.

But Jesus says, "I see good in you.

You can be my helper too."

at **Home**

Jesus saw a gift in Peter that Peter did not see in himself. Think about your young child. What gifts does she or he bring to your family? With your child, talk about the gifts of each family member. How can you use your gifts together to be helpers of Jesus?

Blessed are You

Jesus came down with them and stood on a level place with a great crowd of the disciples and a great multitude of people from all Judea, Jerusalem, and the coast of Tyre and Sidon. . . . Jesus looked up at the disciples and said: "Blessed are you who are poor, for yours is the realm of God. Blessed are you who are hungry now, for you will be filled. Blessed are you who weep now, for you will laugh."

Luke 6:17, 20-21

Marina Silva, *The Beautitudes*, detail, 1981, from *The Gospel in Art by the Peasants of Solitiname*, ed. Philip and Sally Scharper (Maryknoll, N.Y.: Orbis Books). Used by permission.

Many people of all ages came to hear Jesus.

Where is **Jesus** in the picture?

How many **people** are in the picture?

When Jesus

When Jesus **touched** the people, things began to change.
"Though things look bad,
he makes things glad."
When Jesus touched people, things began to **change.**

The Beatitudes: An Echo Drama

And Jesus talked to the people and said,
(Hold hands to mouth.)

"Even though things look bad,
(Gently cover eyes, then pull hands away.)

I am there with you.
(Hug self.)

**Though you may be hurting,
I will hold you and help you.**
(Put arm on another's shoulder.)

**Though you may be hungry,
I will feed you.**
(Hand on stomach, then hand to mouth.)

**Though you may be sad,
I will make you laugh.**
(Frown; with fingers, push frown to a smile.)

**Though you feel left out,
I will wrap you in my arms.**
(Wrap arms around self.)

I won't leave you all alone.
(Form a circle holding hands.)

Rejoice and leap for joy!"
(Leap for joy.)

Sometimes I Feel Sad and Small

Sometimes I feel sad and small

And don't feel any love at all.

But Jesus says, "I see the good.

Can you?

God is always with you too."

at Home

The lesson for the children for Epiphany 6 on the Beatitudes as recorded in Luke 6 focused on verses 20-23a. During this week, act out the Beatitudes echo drama with your child. You both may find reason to "rejoice ...and leap for joy" (Luke 6:23a). Have your child tell the Bible story using the clothes pin figure.

No Strings Attached

Then Joseph said to his brothers, "Come closer to me." And they came closer. He said, "I am your brother, Joseph, whom you sold into Egypt. And now do not be distressed, or angry with yourselves, because you sold me here; for God sent me before you to preserve life."

Genesis 45:4-5

Jacob gave Joseph a beautiful coat.

The
Story
of
Joseph

In Egypt Joseph was in charge of growing and storing grain.

Joseph was happy to see his brothers again.

When God

When God is with people, things begin to change.

Though things look bad,

God makes things glad.

When God is with people, things begin to change.

at **Home**

Telling stories from the Bible to your child is one of the most important ways that you encourage the growth of faith in your child. Tell them as naturally as you would a fairy tale or a story from your childhood. A side effect for you may be gaining a broader knowledge of the Bible. If you are uncertain about how to begin, these resources will be helpful:

- Anderson, Craig V. *Talking With Your Child About the Bible*. Cleveland: United Church Press, 1992.

- Harle-Mould, Linda M., and Hope Douglas J. Harle-Mould. *Talking With Your Child About God's Story*. Cleveland: United Church Press, 1993.

- *The Lion Story Bible*. Belleville, Mich.: Lion Publishing Corporation. Books of single stories, thirty from the Old Testament and twenty-two from the New Testament, retold for young children.

Transfigured

Jesus took with him Peter and John and James, and went up on the mountain to pray. And while Jesus was praying, the appearance of his face changed, and his clothes became dazzling white . . . . Then from the cloud came a voice that said, "This is my Child, my Chosen; to this one you shall listen." When the voice had spoken, Jesus was found alone. And they kept silent and in those days and told no one of the things they had seen.

Luke 9:28b-29, 35-36

High on the Mountaintop

Jesus went up to the mountain one day.
He wanted a quiet place to pray.
He went with Peter and James and John,
But all his other friends were gone.

They prayed with Jesus, then took a break.
They had a hard time staying awake.
Jesus asked God what he needed to do
To show others God's glory too.

Then his clothes changed to a brilliant white
And from his face shown a dazzling light.
Suddenly two others did appear;
his friends woke up and saw them there.

They saw Moses who gave the law, you know,
And Elijah a prophet from long ago.

Then a cloud came and covered them;
A voice said, "This is my child, listen to him!"
The cloud went away. Jesus was now alone.
He called to his disciples, "It's time to go home."

When Jesus

A Prayer Based on Psalm 99:8-9

O God, Our God,
Thank you that you listen to our prayers,
That you give us good things,
That you forgive us when we make mistakes.
We praise you, God,
And worship you on this sacred mountain
and everywhere. Amen.

When Jesus is with people,

things begin to change.

Things turn bright

With God's special light.

When Jesus is with people,

things begin to change.

I Am the Light of the World

Words: Howard Thurman and Jim Strathdee

Music: Jim Strathdee

"I am the light of the world! You peo-ple come and fol-low me!" If you fol-low and love you'll learn the mys-ter-y of what you were meant to do and be.

Words and music copyright © 1969 by Jim Strathdee, Desert Flower Music, Ridgecrest, CA. Used by permission.

at Home

If your child is exhausted from church school today, it is because we climbed a mountain. As you tell Bible stories to your child, look for ways to act them out as we did today. Ask your child about the experience. The song we sang as we hiked up the mountain was "I Am the Light of the World" on this learner's guide. Sing it together.

Meeting Temptation

Jesus, in the wilderness,

was tempted.

Luke 4:1-2a

Jesus was tempted and said **"no."**

I Want Jesus to Walk With Me

Words: African-American spiritual

African-American spiritual

I want Je - sus to walk with me;

I want Je - sus to walk with me;

▶ *at* **Home**

During Lent, we will be marking the days until Easter with a special Lenten calendar. With your child, mark off the days from Ash Wednesday to Easter, to help your child gain a sense of the building excitement toward this great festival day of the church.

For the next few weeks, we will close our time together as a church school group by singing "I Want Jesus to Walk with Me." The children are learning the first two lines of this African-American spiritual. If you have the Word Among Us, Year One cassette, listen to the entire song with your child. Sing the two lines above together.

Challenged

Jesus said, "Jerusalem, Jerusalem,
how I wish I could gather your
children together as a hen gathers
her chickens under her wings!"

Luke 13:34

Jesus went to Jerusalem, a city he loved,
and wished he could help all its people.

We can do God's work, too.

✳ *at* **Home**

Include your child in things you do for others this week. Our children learn what God's work is by participating in it with us.

The stories of the lectionary during Lent are difficult ones for young children, perhaps even for adults. During this season, we will stress the ways that Jesus teaches us about God and God's love. Share your faith with your child as you pray and participate in the ministry of your congregation.

Talk about people in your town or city who need help. Do they, or you, know any stories of the helpers? Find newspaper pictures of helpers and cut them out together.

Free to Rejoice

"Woman, you are set free from your ailment." When Jesus healed her, immediately she began praising God.

Luke 13:13

Jesus healed the sick woman and she began praising God.

This is the Day

Words: anonymous; alt. 1983   Music: Fiji Islands folk melody

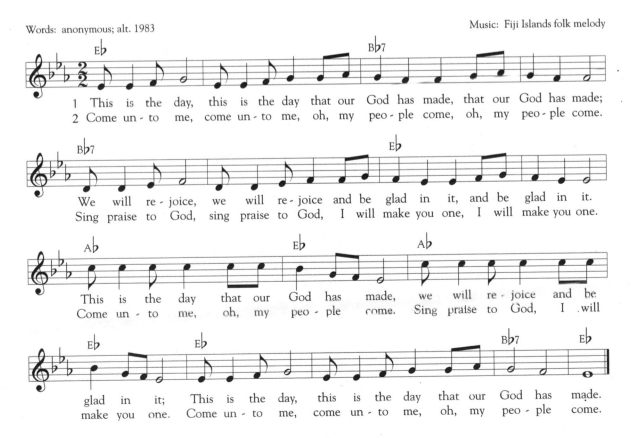

1 This is the day, this is the day that our God has made, that our God has made;
2 Come un-to me, come un-to me, oh, my peo-ple come, oh, my peo-ple come.

We will re-joice, we will re-joice and be glad in it, and be glad in it.
Sing praise to God, sing praise to God, I will make you one, I will make you one.

This is the day that our God has made, we will re-joice and be
Come un-to me, oh, my peo-ple come. Sing praise to God, I will

glad in it; This is the day, this is the day that our God has made.
make you one. Come un-to me, come un-to me, oh, my peo-ple come.

Jesus Healed a Woman

Judith Oelfke Smith, *Jesus Freeing Crippled Woman*, 1993, commissioned work. Used by permission.

at **Home**

Ask your child to tell you the Bible story for today. Recall together times when your family has been very happy. Give thanks to God for such times.

Young children are often curious about people who look different from them, especially older adults who may have physical disabilities. Hearing this story about the woman who could not stand up straight may bring questions about persons they know who have physical handicaps. Answer their questions honestly. Provide opportunities for them to get to know older adults, especially if their grandparents are not nearby.

Welcome Home

While the younger son was still far off, his father saw him and was filled with compassion; he ran and put his arms around him and kissed him.

Luke 15:20

Rembrandt van Rijn,
*The Return of the
Prodigal Son*, 1636,
The Hermitage Museum,
St. Petersburg, Russia
(Scala/Art Resource, N.Y.).
Used by permission.

Look at each person in the painting.

How do you think each one **feels**?

a Rhyme about
My Family

Use the following finger play to make up a rhyme about your family. You can add as many lines as there are persons in your family. You may even want to include a grandparent or a family pet. See how many ways you can say your rhyme.

This is a mother.
(point to the thumb)

This is a brother.
(point to the pointer finger)

This is a sister tall.
(point to the middle finger)

This is a grandfather.
(point to the ring finger)

This is a baby.
(point to the little finger)

Oh, how God loves them all.
(wrap arms around chest as in a hug)

at **Home**

Have your child tell you the story of "Welcome Home."
Look together at the picture and talk about how it feels to leave and return.

The story today about the forgiving father is one you can tell many times to your child at bedtime, anytime you are waiting for someone, or when walking somewhere together. Read it in Luke 15:11b-32. Tell stories from the Bible as naturally as you would a fairy tale. Let your child know that the stories are important to you too.

Jesus or the Poor?

Mary took perfume, washed Jesus' feet, and wiped them with her hair. The house was filled with the sweet smell of the perfume.

John 12:3-5, 7-8

Mary welcomed Jesus by pouring sweet smelling perfume on his dusty feet.

How do you welcome friends to your house?

Welcome!

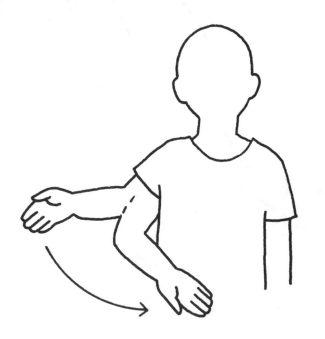

✏ *at* **Home**

Look for ways to include your child in welcoming friends and relatives to your home. Will you be having company during the next two weeks? Perhaps your child can have a role in cleaning the house or preparing a special dessert. Your child might enjoy making a welcome sign for the guest.

Palm Branches
and a Cross

"The whole crowd began to praise God joyfully
with a loud voice, saying, "Blessed is Jesus who
comes in the name of God!"

Luke 19:37b-38a

"Hosanna!"
"Alleluia!"
The people welcomed **Jesus** to **Jerusalem.**

Who do you see in this picture?
How do you know which person is **Jesus?**

71

Loud Hosannas Let Us Sing

Words: Gertrude Priester, 1979

Music: attributed to Robert Williams, 1817

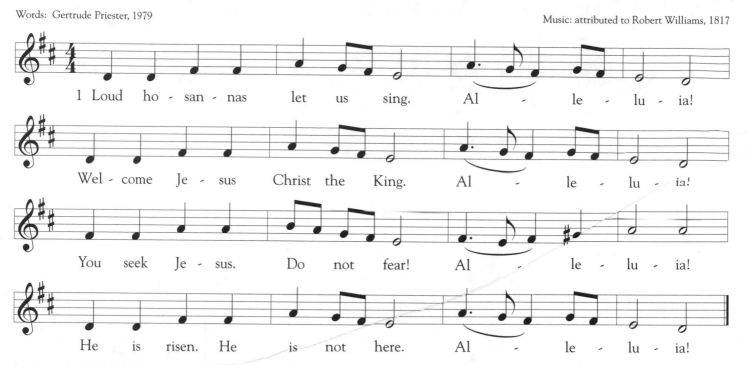

1 Loud ho-san-nas let us sing. Al - le - lu - ia!

Wel - come Je - sus Christ the King. Al - le - lu - ia!

You seek Je - sus. Do not fear! Al - le - lu - ia!

He is risen. He is not here. Al - le - lu - ia!

From *Interpreting the Word, Year II — Spring*, Beta Book 7. Words copyright © 1979 by The Geneva Press. Used by permission.

❖ *at* **Home**

With your child, plan ways for your family to celebrate the joy of Easter. You might plan the menu for Easter dinner together or create a special table or window decoration.

Today the children learned the first two lines of the hymn "Loud Hosannas Let Us Sing." On Easter they will learn the rest of it. Sing it together during the week.

Young children often have questions about Easter and Jesus' death. Answer the questions simply and honestly, according to your faith. Assure them of your love and of God's care.

Weep No More

Jesus said to Mary Magdalene, "Woman, why are you weeping? Whom are you looking for?" Supposing Jesus to be the gardener, she answered, "Sir, if you have carried Jesus away, tell me where you have laid him, and I will take him away." Jesus said to her, "Mary!" She turned responded in Hebrew, "Rabbouni!" (which means Teacher).

John 20:15-16

Albert P. Ryder, *Christ Appearing to Mary*. Gift of John Gellatly, National Museum of American Art, Smithsonian Institution (Art Resource, N.Y.). Used by permission.

Mary went to tell Jesus' friends that she had seen him.

Who have **you** told about Jesus?

From **Palm Sunday** to **Easter**

at **Home**

The celebration of Easter may not lend itself to the experience of children as easily as Christmas, but even young children can be included in the joyous celebration. Celebrate this day in your home with a special meal or table centerpiece.

Have your child help you tell the story of Mary at the empty tomb. The pictures here will help you both.

Loud Hosannas Let Us Sing

Words: Gertrude Priester, 1979   Music: attributed to Robert Williams, 1817

2 Christ our Lord is here to-day. Al - le - lu - ia!

Lis - ten now to what we say! Al - le - lu - ia!

Christ our Lord is risen to - day! Al - le - lu - ia!

Hear our prais - es as we say Al - le - lu - ia!

Peace Be with You

The doors of the house where the disciples met were locked, but Jesus appeared and stood among them and said, "Peace be with you."

John 20:19

Michael Smither, *Doubting Thomas*, St. Joseph's Church, New Plymouth, New Zealand.
Used by permission of Asian Christian Art Association, Kyoto, Japan.

Thomas did not believe his friends. But he did believe Jesus.

Peace

We can work together to bring peace to others.

Can you find these things hidden in the picture?

at Home

As the season of Eastertide continues, the children will continue to hear stories about Jesus. You can reinforce these stories by telling them to your child in your own words. From time to time, invite your child to tell a story about Jesus to you as well.

Hang the poster your child made in a place of honor in your home. How can you make peacemaking a priority in your family life? What special things does your church do that could be called "peacemaking"? How can your family participate in these activities?

Come, Have Breakfast

When they had gone ashore, they saw a charcoal fire
there, with fish on it, and bread. Jesus said to them,
"Bring some of the fish that you have just caught."
So Simon Peter went aboard and hauled the net
ashore, full of large fish, a hundred fifty-three of them;
and though there were so many, the net was not torn.
Jesus said to them, "Come and have breakfast."

John 21:9-12a

Who are the **people** in this picture?

Can you tell a **story** about this picture?

🐟 *at* **Home**

Have your child tell the story for today using the fishing pole and fish.

Look for ways that you and your child can follow Jesus by helping others. Is there a friend or relative to whom you can send a cheerful note along with a drawing by your child? Or can you bake muffins or cookies for a shelter or food pantry, a nursing home, or a day-care center? Why not go through clothes together and take those your child has outgrown to a clothes closet or thrift shop?

Shepherd Psalm

God is my shepherd, I shall not want.

Psalm 23:1

The **shepherd**

knows **each**

sheep by **name,**

and **watches** over them

carefully.

Psalm 23

God is my shepherd;

I shall not want.

God makes me lie down in green pastures;

God leads me beside still waters;

God restores my soul.

God leads me in right paths.

The Good Shepherd, c. 250 C.E., in Cubiculum Velatio, Catacomb of Priscilla, Rome. Used by permission of Commissione Pontificiale per Archeologia Sacra, Città Vaticano, Italy (Alinari/Art Resource, N.Y.). Used by permission.

at Home

Each child is precious and loved by God just as each sheep is loved by the shepherd. This week look for the uniqueness of your child and praise those qualities. Express by your actions how much you love your child. Be a good shepherd to him or her.

The children said the rewritten version of selected verses of Psalm 23 on the learner's guide several times during "The Liturgy of Learning" today. Say it with your child throughout this week. You will be surprised at how quickly your child will learn these verses.

Although young children have little understanding of symbol or metaphor, they can begin to gain an impression about the trust they can put in God. This trust is the very foundation of faith. Help your child build that trust in God through trusting you. Your child will begin to connect trust with you and your trust in God if you pray with your child, not only listening to your child's prayers.

A Family Prayer

Dear God, we believe in you.

Thank you for each person in our family.

Pause for each person to name a family member.

During this day, help us remember that you are with us.

Name things that will happen during the day.

Amen.

All Things New

Choi Hyun-Joo, *Jerusalem*, 1976, in *Children of the World Paint Jerusalem* (New York: Bantam Book/published by arrangement with Keter Publishing House Jerusalem Ltd., 1978). Used by permission.

How does the picture make you feel?

What is surprising or new about this picture?

What in the picture reminds you of love or peace?

Then I saw a new heaven and a new earth. And I heard a loud voice from the throne saying, "God will indeed be with them and will wipe every tear from their eyes. See, I am making all things new."

Revelation 21:1, 3-5a

For all God's children, a world of

Peace!

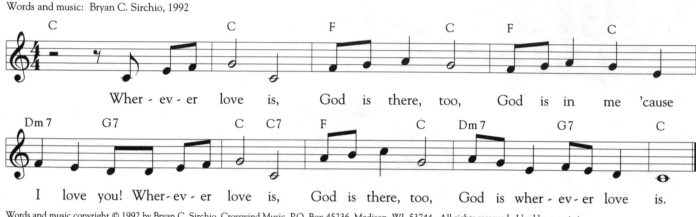

Dr. Martin Luther King, Jr., had a dream

that everyone would live together in peace.

Wherever Love Is

Words and music: Bryan C. Sirchio, 1992

Wher-ev-er love is, God is there, too, God is in me 'cause I love you! Wher-ev-er love is, God is there, too, God is wher-ev-er love is.

at Home

A reading from The Revelation to John may seem an unusual choice for young children. However, in *Word Among Us* everyone is engaged with the same lectionary reading. Actually, the vision presented in this reading is one that we all need to hear, especially young children. Children today hear of the world's tragedies at an earlier age than we may imagine. To learn that the church, parents, and friends are working to make a better world, one that is true to God's vision, is comforting knowledge.

During the week join your child in activities that will make your home and neighborhood a better place. Things you might do are:

- pick up the trash in your neighborhood
- plant flowers
- assist a neighbor who needs help
- clean up a nearby park

Help your child think of things that you can do to make the world a better place in which to live and play.

Open Heart, Open Home

A certain woman named Lydia, a worshiper of God, was listening to us; she was from the city of Thyatira and a dealer in purple cloth. God opened her heart to listen eagerly to what was said by Paul.

Acts 16:14

Lydia listened carefully to Paul's teachings about Jesus. She believed in Jesus and welcomed Paul and his friends to her home.

We Are the Church

I am the church!
Point to self.

You are the church!
Point to someone else.

We are the church together!
Take hands to make a circle.

All who follow Jesus,
Walk around a circle as you finish the rhyme.

All around the world!

Yes, we're the church together!

Richard Avery. © 1967 by Hope Publishing Company, Carol Stream, IL 60188.
All rights reserved. Used by permission.

Little Children, Welcome

Words: Fred Pratt Green, 1973

Music: Roy Hopp, 1988

Lit - tle chil - dren, wel - come! Earth is yours to live in;

arms of love pro - tect you, lit - tle chil - dren, wel - come!

at **Home**

Help your child think of ways to be hospitable to guests as Lydia was when she opened her home to Paul and his friends. Prepare for a guest or guests together. Talk about ways to make guests feel at home.

Think of people who could be invited to go to church with you. If you are invited to be a greeter on Sunday morning, include your children in that experience.

Connections

One day, as we were going to the place of prayer, we met a slave-girl who had a spirit of divination and brought her owners a great deal of money by fortune-telling. ...But when her owners saw that their hope of making money was gone, they seized Paul and Silas and dragged them into the marketplace before the authorities.

Acts 16:16, 19

Good news leads to good works.

Look how happy the people are in this picture.

Can you find Paul and Silas?
Which person do you think is the jailer?
What has made everyone so happy?

Good news

for all Children

When Marian Wright Edelman was a little girl, she helped her parents take food to families who were hungry. Her father was the pastor of a church. He and her mother built a playground for the African American children because they were not allowed to play where the white children played. They also began a home for older people who had no one to care for them.

Marian and her brothers and sister learned about Jesus from their parents. They also learned how to help others as Jesus taught.

Today Marian Wright Edelman is the head of a group called the Children's Defense Fund. She believes that all children should have healthy food, a safe home, and persons who love them. She works for this because her parents taught her about Jesus and treated her this way.

See Marian Wright Edelman, *The Measure of Our Success: A Letter to My Children and Yours* (Boston: Beacon Press, 1992).

at Home

This lesson concludes the season of Easter. Go over the stories for these weeks with your child.

The children heard two stories today that suggested the connection between faith and action. The focus scripture tells of faith put into action by Paul and Silas. The contemporary story about Marian Wright Edelman is on this learner's guide.

Help your children explore their actions and words. Although it is premature to talk of a child relating faith to action, young children can be involved with us as we do that on a more mature level. You might help a neighbor plant some flowers or clean up the area around the church building. If your congregation collects food for a food bank, take your child with you when you shop for the food or deliver it. If your church does not collect food, perhaps your family can investigate the possibility of making your church building a collection point.

Pentecost Is Coming!

Next Sunday is Pentecost.
Wear something red.
You'll find out why next week.

Pentecost's Many
Voices

On the day of Pentecost all of them were filled with the Holy Spirit and began to speak in other languages, as the Spirit gave them ability.

Acts 2:1-2, 4

Emil Nolde, *The Pentecost*, 1909, Stiftung Seebull, Ada und Emil Nolde, Neukirchen. Used by permission.

The **Holy Spirit** came to Jesus' friends on Pentecost Day.

Who do you think the person is with both hands on the table?

What story can you tell about this picture?

at **Home**

Today, Pentecost, is the birthday of the church. We celebrated the nearly two thousand years of the Christian church today with a birthday cake. Why not continue the celebration in your family? Sing "Happy Birthday" to the church together. On this special day in the life of the church, see how many ways you can help the church celebrate. Maybe you and your child could bake birthday cupcakes and take some to a neighbor or an older member of your church who lives alone.

Make birthday cards to send to friends in other congregations or to special friends in your own congregation.

Hope Given

Hope does not disappoint us.

Romans 5:5

Seed Wonder

I am very, very tiny;
You can hold me in your hand
And look at me quite closely
But still not understand
Just what there is inside of me
That makes me grow and grow
When I am planted in the ground
With others in a row.

Soon you'll see green slender shoots
Break through the garden bed,
And baby buds will then appear,
Each lifting up its head
To drink the rain and catch the sun
Until it opens wide
To show the lovely fragrant flower
That God has wrapped inside.

Mable Niedermeyer McCaw, from Pictures and Stories,
© 1959 by The Methodist Publishing House. Used by permission.

from **Seed** to **Flower**

Hope is trusting there is a future.

at **Home**

An abstract theological term like hope is not an easy one to interpret to children. In church school today we chose to use the cycle of growth to help the children understand that we can trust in a future because we can trust in God.

Help your child care for the seed we planted today. Talk together about what it needs—just enough sun and water—and how God planned it that way. Read the poem "Seed Wonder" together. Look for other things that are growing.

A children's book about plants growing that you and your child might enjoy is *The Carrot Seed* by Ruth Krauss (Harper & Row, 1945). Look for it at your library.

An Alabaster Jar

Jesus said to the woman,
"You are forgiven."

Luke 7:48

What

can you tell about the woman
with the alabaster jar
from this picture?

Who

are the other people
in the picture?

?

Wu Yuen-kwei, *Her Sins Are Forgiven*, The Asian Christian Art Association,
Sakyo-ku, Kyoto, Japan. Used by permission.

Welcome, Welcome

How do you welcome friends to your house?
Complete the picture on the right
to show how you say "welcome" to a guest.

at **Home**

Even at the tender age of four or five, your child has sought
your forgiveness many times. Although your child may not
understand the nuances of social class, sin, or religious hier-
archy that can be found in the story of the woman with the
alabaster jar, your child does know what it means to be
loved and forgiven. You are the person who teaches that
simple but profound lesson day after day after day. Keep it
up for you are helping your child learn the magnitude of
God's love.

Many children's books deal with love and forgiveness.
One that is especially enjoyable to read with a child is
Even If I Did Something Awful by Barbara Shook Hazen
(New York: The Macmillan Company, 1981). Look for
it in your library and read it together.

One in Christ

All of you are one in Christ Jesus.

Galatians 3:28b

You are one in Jesus.

Norman Rockwell, *The Golden Rule*, © The Curtis Publishing Company.
1961, The Norman Rockwell Museum of Stockbridge, Massachusetts.
Used by permission.

How many different kinds of people can you find in this picture?

Can you find someone who is very old?

Someone who is very young?

Someone who is from another country?

A Song to Thank God

Sung to "Are You Sleeping?"

God, we thank you. God, we thank you.
For our food. For our food.
How we like to eat it. How we like to eat it.
Thank you, God. Thank you, God.

at **Home**

Today we talked about belonging to Jesus. When we belong to Jesus, we welcome all others in Jesus' name. During these summer weeks, look for ways to introduce your child to persons who are different from you. Go to street fairs in ethnic neighborhoods. Visit special exhibits about other countries at museums. Take every opportunity to introduce your child to the wealth of persons God included in creation.

Your child might enjoy learning about other people by reading *People* by Peter Spier (Doubleday, 1980) with you.

Freedom to Love and Serve

"You shall love your neighbor as yourself."

Galatians 5:14

Paul wrote to many new churches.

He wanted them to remember what

Jesus taught. What is something you

remember that Jesus taught?

Through love serve one another.

at **Home**

In church school, we have been talking about loving our neighbors and what that can mean in our lives. Jesus taught us to love our neighbor as we love ourselves. What can that mean to you and your child? Perhaps together you and your child can think of ways to help your neighbors. Talk about the suggestions pictured on this learner's guide. Remember that neighbors do not need to live nearby. Neighbors can also be family members. Can you and your child find a way to make a difference in another person's life?

Next week we will be talking about things that make your child feel comfortable. Help your child choose something that makes him or her feel good, such as a special blanket, pillow, or stuffed animal, to bring to church school.

Love Your Neighbor

As a Mother Comforts Her Child

As a mother comforts her child,
so I will comfort you.

Isaiah 66:13

God comforts us

as a mother comforts her child.

Mary Cassatt, *Margot Embracing Her Mother
(Mother and Child)*, 1902, gift of Ms. Aimee Lamb
in memory of Mr. and Mrs. Horatio A. Lamb,
Museum of Fine Arts, Boston. Used by permission.

Rejoice with Jerusalem!

(Based on Isaiah 66:10-14)

Be glad for Jerusalem!
God said to Jerusalem,
"As a mother cares for her child,
I will care for you.
You will rejoice.
You shall grow tall.
Everyone will know that
God is with you."
Rejoice with Jerusalem!

at Home

The images of God that young children develop are fascinating indeed. Not long ago a four-year-old boy was prompted to look at the clouds by his father, who was sorely tried in his efforts to entertain the young lad, this being the final leg of the flight from Seattle to Newark.

"I see God," said the boy. His father made no comment. The boy turned to him and said, "No, that's not right. God's in my heart."

Another four-year-old said, in no particular conversational context, "God is everywhere. God is all over and inside us at the same time."

Rather than tell your child about God, listen to your child tell you about God this week. Ask questions: Where is God? What do you think God is like? Do you ever talk to God?

Hard Words

Then Amos answered Amaziah, "I am no prophet, nor a prophet's son; but I am a herdsman, and a dresser of sycamore trees, and God took me from following the flock, and God said to me, 'Go prophesy to my people Israel.'"

Amos 7:14-15

"I am no prophet, but God took me from my farm and said, **'Go speak to my people.'"**

Amos and Amaziah

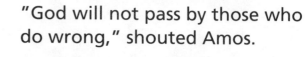

"God will not pass by those who do wrong," shouted Amos.

Amaziah answered, "Go to Judah! Speak your words from God there! We don't want to hear you here!"

"I am no prophet, but a farmer. God took me from my land to bring this message to you. Listen to what I say!" called Amos.

What do you think will happen next?

Will Amos stay?

at **Home**

The little story from Amos is summarized in the three lines of "Amos and Amaziah." However, as is often the case, the message behind those three lines is an important one. Amos, "a herdsman, and a dresser of sycamore trees," was plucked from his ordinary life to be God's prophet to God's people. Ask your child to tell the story using the puppet made during church school today.

While each of us, child or adult, may not be given such a demanding task, we too are chosen by God. What is it that God has called you to do? What is it that God has called your family to do?

Justice for the Poor

God said to Amos, "I will never forget their unjust deeds."

Amos 8:7

Amos **warned** the people that they were forgetting God's ways.

 How are the **children** in this picture doing what God wants?

Helping Our Friends

Make up your own finger rhyme. Complete each line by naming something you will be gathering to help other families.

The children in the church school group are working to help others. One brought in one
Hold up one finger.

Two brought in two
Hold up two fingers.

Three brought in three
Hold up three fingers.

Four brought in four
Hold up four fingers.

Five brought in five
Hold up four fingers and the thumb.

DON'T FORGET! Bring this to church school next week!

at **Home**

Ask your child to tell you about the project for others we began today after hearing the story about Amos. Amos told the Israelites to follow God's way and to help those who are poor.

Complete the finger rhyme on this learner's guide together.

Help your child remember to bring the item written on the box above, though your child may well be the one to remind you!

The Prayer of Jesus

▲ Jesus was praying in a certain place, and after he had finished, one of the disciples said to him, "Jesus, teach us to pray."

Luke 11:1

Albrecht Dürer, *Study of Hands in Adoration*, c. 1509. The Albertina, Vienna (Foto Marburg/Art Resource, N.Y.). Used by permission.

▲ **Sometimes we pray with our hands like this.**

▲ **How else do we pray?**

A Prayer of Jesus

Our Father [and Mother],
who is in heaven,
Holy is your name.
Your world come.
Your will be done,
On earth as it is in heaven.

Matthew 6:9-10

at **Home**

As in so much of what young children learn, you are the model for your child. When do your children see or hear you pray? Have all mealtime prayers been relegated to the children in your family? Only as children hear and see you pray will they understand the importance and power of prayer in the lives of the followers of Jesus.

Pray together "A Prayer of Jesus." When it is your turn to pray at a mealtime, say the prayer as you have learned it. Help your children appreciate the widespread use of this prayer, in its many forms, around the world.

In God's Arms

God said to Israel, "I taught you to walk, I took you up in my arms.
I bent down to you and fed you."

Hosea 11:3-4

As closely as

this parent

hugs the child

does GOD

hold us.

William Taylor, *Mother and Child*, 1962, collection of the artist.
Reproduced in David C. Driskell, *Two Centuries of Black
American Art* (New York: Los Angeles County Museum of Art/
Alfred A. Knopf, 1976), 204.

GOD

is always ready

to welcome us

with open arms.

at **Home**

Young children are realists. They learn to understand abstract concepts such as love and God by the experiences that they have each day. *You* are the most important person in teaching your child about God and God's love. And how you understand God is instrumental in how you teach your child. In *Christian Parenting*, the authors are clear about this connection as they describe why they wrote the book:

> *Our most important reason for daring to take this on is our desire to help parents make the connection between the everyday process of parenting and their faith. We believe very strongly that the way parents raise children is inextricably bound up with their theology. If we view God as a stern judge, and base our theology on a punishment model ("If you're not good, you won't get to Heaven") our parenting will reflect that.*
>
> *But if we view God as a loving co-creator, then our parenting will reflect that attitude, too. We must encourage our children to think for themselves; everyone has responsibility for helping a family function well together.*

Donna Sinclair and Yvonne Steward, *Christian Parenting: Raising Children in the Real World* (Louisville: Westminster/John Knox Press, 1992), 6.

By Faith

Faith is the assurance of things hoped for.

Hebrews 11:1

God promised Abraham and Sarah many children,
grandchildren, and great-grandchildren. God told them there
would be as many as there are stars in the sky.

How many stars are there in the sky in this picture?

Faith, the assurance of things hoped for, the conviction of things not seen. Without realizing it, your child begins and ends each day exhibiting great faith in you. The trust that your child is able to place in you can form the basis for your child's faith in God. You are your child's primary teacher of the Christian faith. As you continue growing in faith so will your child grow.

Although the scripture for Pentecost 10 is from Hebrews, the children heard part of the story of Abraham and Sarah, to whom the writer of Hebrews points as our ancestors in faith. Say the poem "Abraham and Sarah" with your child. Tell your child about ancestors in faith who are important to you, including those who are still alive. Look at the stars one clear night this week.

Sarah and Abraham

Sarah and Abraham were people of God.

They had faith.

They listened to God's words.

They had faith.

God promised them a new land.

They had faith.

They left their home and traveled far.

They had faith.

God promised them many children.

They had faith.

They got older and older.

They had faith.

Though she was older than a grandmother,

They had faith.

Sarah had baby Isaac, later Jacob too!

They had faith.

Sarah and Abraham were people of God.

They had faith.

We are people of God

We have faith, too.

The Cloud of Witnesses

We are surrounded by so great a cloud of witnesses.

Hebrews 12:1

Judith Oelfke Smith, *Jesus Freeing Crippled Woman*, 1993, commissioned work. Used by permission.

The Good Shepherd, c. 250 C.E., in Cubiculum Velatio, Catacomb of Priscilla, Rome. Used by permission of Commissione Pontificiale per Archeologia Sacra, Città Vaticano, Italy (Alinari/Art Resource, N.Y.). Used by permission.

These are some of the persons you heard about this year.

Which ones can you tell a story about?

at Home

Today we tried to remember as many of the persons we have talked about this year as we could. Some of them are pictured on this learner's guide. How many can you and your child identify? To help you if you get stuck, see the diagram below with the names and scripture references.

We also talked about people today who are part of the "cloud of witnesses" who help us know what it is to be the church. Who would you add to the cloud? Tell your child a story about someone who has helped you learn about God or how to be a follower of Jesus.

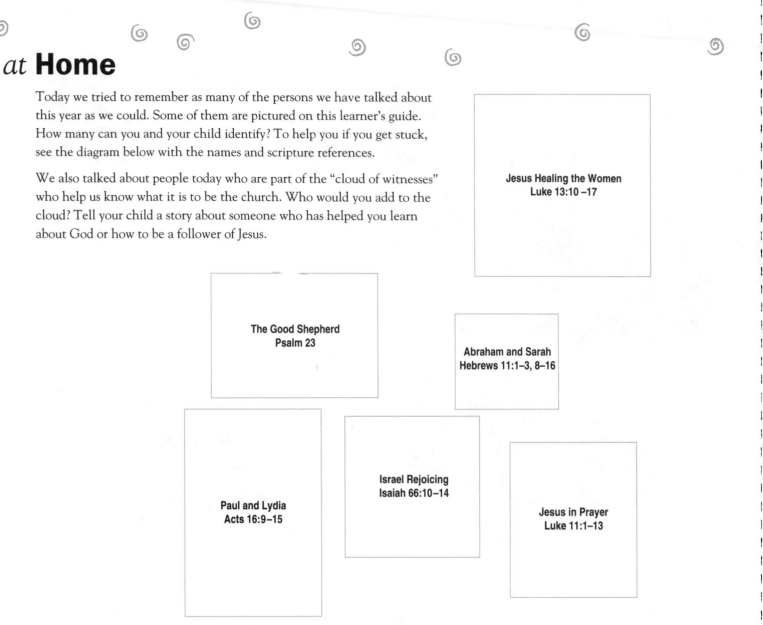

Jesus Healing the Women
Luke 13:10–17

The Good Shepherd
Psalm 23

Abraham and Sarah
Hebrews 11:1–3, 8–16

Paul and Lydia
Acts 16:9–15

Israel Rejoicing
Isaiah 66:10–14

Jesus in Prayer
Luke 11:1–13

The Cloud of Witnesses

Words adapted from Evelyn M. Andre   Music: source unknown

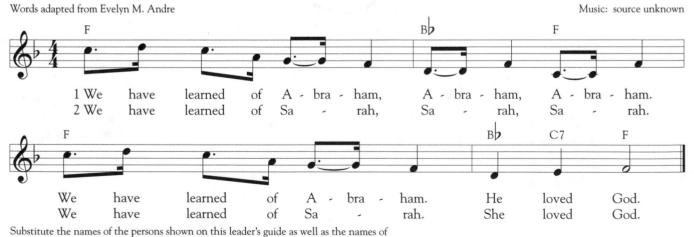

1 We have learned of A-bra-ham, A-bra-ham, A-bra-ham.
2 We have learned of Sa-rah, Sa-rah, Sa-rah.

We have learned of A-bra-ham. He loved God.
We have learned of Sa-rah. She loved God.

Substitute the names of the persons shown on this leader's guide as well as the names of people you know in the church and members of your family.

All That Is Within Me
–Bless God

Jonathan Green, *The Congregation*, detail, 1991,
Jonathan Green Studios, Inc., Naples, Fla.
Used by permission.

Bless God, O my soul,
and all that is within me,
bless God's holy name.

Psalm 103:1, 8

Bless God, Oh My Soul

Words: Ps. 103:1, 8
Adapted by Russell E. Sonafrank, II, 1988; alt.

Music: Stephen J. Morris, 1988

Response

Bless God, O my soul! All with - in me bless God's name!

Bless God, who was, and is, and shall ev - er be the same!

! ! ! ! ! ! ! ! ! *at* **Home**

Who can better praise God with their whole bodies than young children? We adults get so involved with the right words and the correct posture. Today we praised God with song and movement. We spent time praising rather than talking about it. Have your child *show* you how we moved to the songs we sang. Ask your child to echo the lines of "Bless God" after you read each one with the joy that we used today. If possible, go outdoors and praise God to the tops of your voices together.

Psalm 103

Bless God

Bless God with all of your body.

Bless God with your head,

your heart,

your hands,

your feet,

your eyes,

your ears,

and your mouth.

Bless God.

Bless God's name.

Do not forget all God has done for you:

God forgives you.

God heals you.

God is good to you.

God loves you.

God will always love you.

God's love will last forever.

God is Good!